For Linda,
with warm,

Faye George
4/28/04

Back Roads

Also by Faye George

———

A Wound on Stone, 2001
Naming the Place: The Weymouth Poems, 1996 (chapbook)
Only the Words, 1995 (chapbook)

Back Roads

Faye George

ROCK VILLAGE PUBLISHING
MIDDLEBOROUGH, MASSACHUSETTS
First Printing

Back Roads

Typography and cover by Ruth Brown

This book is set in Minion, a type family designed in 1990 by Robert Slimbach for Adobe, Inc., specifically for digital composition technology. The type is a contemporary interpretation of classical Renaissance letterforms.

Poems in this collection originally appeared
in the following publications:

THE AMICUS JOURNAL: "Shagbark," "Wilderness"
THE CHRISTIAN SCIENCE MONITOR: "Door to Door"
IBBETSON STREET: "Chickens"
INTERIM: "Back River," "Breakfast at Sarni's"
THE LARCOM REVIEW: "A Diner Closed"
THE MIDWEST QUARTERLY: "Birthday"
POET LORE: "A Place in the Woods"
POETRY: "Like Anne Shirley's House," "Night Piece," "Plum"
THE PROVIDENCE JOURNAL: "Wickford"
SANCTUARY: "Kramer's Farm"
SOUTH SHORE MAGAZINE: "Tidal Marsh"
YANKEE: "Back Roads," "Bits of Things Falling Away,"
        "Indian Summer," "Invitation," "Tenant at Will"

Front Cover: Wickford Village, Rhode Island

ISBN 0-9721389-3-5

Rock Village Publishing
41 Walnut Street
Middleborough MA 02346
(508) 946-4738

For Reed and Laurel

CONTENTS

ROOMS WE HAVE LIVED IN

ROOMS WE HAVE LIVED IN

BACK ROADS

That country inn where you stopped for lunch
and stayed the afternoon when you were half
way to where you thought—remember it?
The woods a mauve haze, the lawn sloping down
to a penciled stream, the Unitarian steeple
promising all shall be well, when you needed faith.

Each time you are half way you go back.
The forward-leaning slant of March prods.
You thirst for the slow melt of April on rock,
of April's deep-shaded roots like the veins
of old hands holding on. You are an old hand,
listening to the whispering tires:
      you are almost there, you are almost there.

TENANT AT WILL

The oak dresser takes its luster
from the brass lamp,
the way sunset pools on Carver Pond.
The grain of the wood flows
across the clutter of this narrow room,
across the routine of my life
in this college town.
It has been nine years
since I came here knocking on doors
until this small house said:

> You may come in.
> I will give you a roof
> and the bedroom wall for your books.
> That is all.
> If you want something more, move on.

I used to envy the geese
who pass over my roof with their ruckus,
until I learned they were only commuting
between the swamp and the pond;
all that fuss to go a few blocks.
But every fall
some break with the local flock,
slicing away old ties
with the soft serration of wings.

WICKFORD

For as long as it might take a really good book
to burn in the hunger of the mind,
a book read again and again with the slow turn of thumb
that leaves an imprint on pages,
I return through photograph albums
up the granite steps and down the path the light took

between honeysuckle and trumpet vine
to the rear of number sixty, the antique colonial
across from St. Paul's,
whose bells thrilled the quiet walls and cellar stones
of Sunday, scattering birds throughout the Village,
and called us from our sleep

in rooms that wore their history
warmed with the scent of our young lives.
The house, eighteenth-century, was yellow and white,
shutters the shade of Christmas balsam.
A house photographed, sketched—
and redrawn again as home, in the firelight of memory:

The lift of the porch to the threshold,
painted pine floors,
rooms furnished in a comfortable muddle
of walnut and maple, wicker and oak,
a frayed oriental, a Jeanne d'Arc monochrome:
castoffs, the envy of any bohemian.

I could find my way blindfold down to the wharf,
naming the old families of Main Street,
their gardens of iris and hollyhock;
and the little shops of the Fifties, in the days of the A & P,
before the Standard Times left the corner
across from Updike Park for the Avis Block.

I go back—
like someone searching the want ads, the personals—
looking for us, when we were us.
Where else can I find us if not there, on the porch,
in the broken light of trumpet vine and honeysuckle,
held in the perfume of the past?

LIKE ANNE SHIRLEY'S HOUSE

I want a house that lifts itself
from the ground with a porch
like the lap of an apron
made to hold me in wicker.
The floor will be fir, clear
vertical grain; cut, milled,
shipped down from the north,
painted over each spring
semigloss gray—deck gray
it will say on the can.

People will come to a porch
composed around
the private dignity of a house
open to friends.

It will have corners for secrets.
The trellised west side
dripping rampant vine, flowering
frantic with bees in July,
a niche for the intimate glance
as amethyst deepens to violet
and the small wild loves of earth
sing out its rhythm
as if the whole country round
were gliding to bliss on rockers.

236 BROAD STREET
for Ken, 12/23/1933-7/6/1990

I saw it last night,
tingling with fireflies,
the old house

full of dust and memories,
the smell of milled wood
through the windows,

the pulse of the hammer
in the journeyman's hand,
the song of the tool

spotting and setting the nail
with the cadence and balance
of dance.

And the green waltz of children
through arborvitae.
I stopped.

The dog heeled,
the old dog
who came out of the high grass,

to return deeply alone
beyond the white pear
where pines soak up sound.

She never barked.
Her eyes held a look so soft
it bit like tooth on bone.

The fireflies blinked,
and the house, like a husk,
fell into the branny dark.

CHRISTMAS EVE AT CONLIN'S

There would be candles
and piano shine, light melting
over wood and shimmering
along the polished boards

to where the edges of the room
dissolved in shadowy canals
the cat patrolled. Out of the dark
an epiphany of balsam.

Mine would be among
the hummock of piled coats,
the promiscuous tangle of scarves,
and voices lyrically merry.

There would be chowder
on the coal-fed range
in the wainscot kitchen,
a crusty bread for dipping,

cheddar and brie,
Baileys and Chivas Regal.
And a place for the regulars
at the kitchen table. Some

would settle in the living room
to watch the fire feed.
The old unblinking monk beside
the telephone in the dining room

would not have shifted his weight
since last I came.
From the heart of the wood,
his solidity holds

something of the soul of this house,
whose people love
what is good, well made,
what is old, having lived.

ORIENTAL RUGS

We have settled them here
on hardwood floors.

Their tones have softened,
the wool balding in places.
But the desert is still in them:

blood red suns,
chilling cobalt skies,
fires in the darkness.

Fixed and coveted,
they possess their space.

ROOMS WE HAVE LIVED IN

He retraces the arrangement of the furniture,
particulars of placement, an indelible detail . . .
The way wicker braided light and shadow
together in the west window,

casting its net across a bare square of floor
to the farthest fringe of the Bokhara,
climbing the wall beyond,
lacing its geometry with an airy art: a screen

imposed upon the woman in the portrait,
as if he glimpsed her again
in the latticed twilight of their first night.
The rooms we have lived in re-enter us

with an isolate clarity. This is what goes on
behind locked eyes in that ghetto where the old go.
He slips away again to let the room come in,
sketching it, like an architect lost in his work.

Bits of Things Falling Away

A bone, a tooth, a button.
From his porch he watches.
They are moving the family grave plot,
having taken the land for the new road
that will link Madison County,
breaking the old connections

that held them together
in the image of one another
folded into the mountain,
bone, tooth, button.

He sees from his place
on the bristled jaw of the mountain
bits of things falling away,
clotted rot-soft pine splintering,
spilling back from the invaded dark
a bone, a tooth, a button.

RHINES LUMBERYARD

The welcoming scent of sawn lumber
— breath of the wood.
The handshake warmly meant as you entered,
when you came for #1 pine, nails
scooped out of a barrel . . .
You believed the place would go on forever
there beside the river, as it had
for as long as any of us and our parents'
parents could remember.

Appearing in old postcard pictures
farther back than that,
when none could have imagined
the buildings gone, ragweed and sumac
filling in between the tracks and wharf
where barges unloaded from the river,
and a new town had sprung.
Or that in its place this scrubby growth
would take over the Yard.

There you'd find the best in the business
down back examining stock
for warps and checks,
who chose with narrowed eye
soffit, fascia, mullion,
when nothing came *pre*cut;
who never thought the day would come
when neither stick nor splinter
would be left to mark the place

where the warehouse stood,
high, rambling, crowding the sidewalk.
It grew as business grew,
leaping the street with a catwalk.
And then became an empty space,
where the fire moved in
to make a proper end,
before something less took over.
It went with its dignity intact,

still wearing the color of bad weather,
the color of its own shadow across Commercial:
puritan gray, dull as an honest man.

BREAKFAST AT SARNI'S

The coffee shop is closed,
but the bus still stops.
With old jokes and headlines
they'd straggle in: Al, Bill,
Bob, Ken—union men.
Jim took off in '78 for Houston.

    I knew
who took his coffee black,
whose toast was dark,
whose eggs were over light,
whose kid had just moved out,
whose wife was mad at him,
who got laid off,
what the business agent
should have told Gilbane,
and why the Red Sox lost
again.

    The awning's gone.
If you stand too close
the sunburned brick
will sting your hand
in the afternoon.

A DINER CLOSED

In case you might have missed the untrimmed shrubs
and broken glass, someone left a message
on that place in East Providence:
THIS HERE'S A DINER CLOSED.

A serious message scrawled to the world
or the few lost souls not from the neighborhood,
who wouldn't have heard. An epitaph,

an obituary for the future of dinerhood,
in the syntax of a country song
Hank Williams could have sung

in his wonderful sorrowful train-whistle moan,
back when diners were as close as we could come
to honky-tonks.

We piled in after the movie for pie a la mode,
Jambalaya and *Kalija* on the jukebox. Rose's, Eddie's—
each as quirky as its one-of-a-kind owner.

Then, the diner went the way of the wooden Indian,
the steam engine, and Hank,
who died too young.

Seeing another headed for oblivion,
padded chrome stools swiveling into some landfill,
is like losing a friend:

this relic on Route 18,
done in by fire, rain, and whatever it is
that gnaws from inside out behind plywood.

Another bit of Art Deco
that took its shape from the railroad,
come to the end of the line.

At Monponsett Inn

The wind is all over itself on the snow
and thick as a tongue on the lake.
One can fill up an afternoon
watching the games of the wind,
the aimless generations of waves
dying along the margins.

I come for the view, the Cabernet
and food affordably good.

It is pleasant in summer to dine on the deck
fanned by a natural breeze,
but I like the cold days
that drive the careering toys off the lake,
when winter returns with its bony arms
full of white flowers.

ROUTE 58

This is the slow road,
the way of least insistence,

running parallel with the railroad tracks
past open fields

and feral orchard remnants.
A road one might easily miss

if thirty-five miles an hour
is not fast enough

through towns sown with gables
and bungalows

where laundry hangs in the sun
and an antique barber pole

day after day
in slow twined rounds

turns among the small shops
with modest signs

framed in the rear view mirror.
A people getting by with just enough,

including clutter.
The unselfconscious yards,

the grace
of well-established trees.

SHOE TOWN

A road no one takes
but the locals and the lost.

Railroad tracks
nothing rides but rust.

An old New England town,
hoary with neglect.

Stopped factories.
Windowless, sooty brick

with the bruised, blinded look
of the fighter who lost.

GLORY HOLE

Ruts fill in over time but you can pick out
the old road through the brush,
a hard-packed swath paved in plantains
that sooner or later branches

in a path to the dump. What you want,
what you came for, is in there,
in the grave of that midden,
which you can't expect to half cover

in the time you have to give. You know
there's nothing in there worth anything,
copper and brass long since culled
and sold for scrap. There are things in there

you really wouldn't want to see again.
You begin anyway, poking first at
the shiny stuff, a chunk of ruby reflector,
Milk-of-Magnesia sapphire,

some Father-John's amber.
Nothing comes whole to the surface.
So what? Bits of blue willowware
still tell their love story.

History spills from the spent worth
of Depression glass, chipped enamelware,
a washboard's galvanized knuckles.
The story of a neighborhood—writ small:

in clam shell and chicken bone,
in the rust lace of old tin, a fragment of rosary,
the Ballantine rings of a family's shame.
A civilization is in there,

molecule and myth: legends abandoned
with the cracked Bakelite of a Philco radio.
You hear the overture. The citizens assemble.
The Lone Ranger rides again . . .

LONE WOLF

Painted by Alfred von Kowalsi-Wierusz

An old friend, he shows up at flea markets,
a study of creature cold and lonely isolation
that hung in Depression Era homes like a mascot.

My Connecticut aunt displayed her print
above the upright in the parlor,
where on summer visits

I returned again and again
to the company of that solitary creature
looking down on a snow-spun cabin

cozy with window light,
smoke rising from the chimney,
the breath of the animal an escaped ghost.

Eyes fixed, glazed from their watch,
he stands as if at the edge of the moon,
guarding his shadow,

muzzle clamped on the howl he does not surrender.
Nothing on that starved hill
in all the snow-blue night but the wolf,

and a faint few crumbs of stars.

112 IRON HILL STREET

City. Branches parted at the sound
of the spoken word, *city.*
Houses of the neighborhood gathered,
interested as aunts who had been there
and returned with secrets in their eyes.
My turn would come, the houses said,
and yes, it would be my adventure—
anointer, hierophant, the city.

The train would be on time,
and the conductor, who would know my name,
could answer all my questions.
I would step forth from the green cave
of the gothic trees and follow the road
that followed the stream, pressing on
toward the port of my city.

CIRCA 1933

Having made your bed in the city
    that helped invent you, coming as you had
        from another country and the times hard,
        you became unnecessary

to the kitchen, the living room,
    the bedroom my mother kept alone.
        As father, you might have been
        any man on a bench in the Common,

face buried in the pages of the *Globe*.
    Only later,
        when you appeared at the door,
        a stranger knowing my name,

letting the flies in, the tiger's eye
    of your Chesterfields filling the room,
        would the questions begin
        that we never found answers to.

I come into the city remembering
    your old haunts under the new,
        a banjo-back chair, a marble-top table ...
        Boston in pentimento,

down-at-the-mouth Boston of the Thirties.
    It was all here for the long-legged democrat
        walking these streets,
        shoes worn to your socks:

the hand to mouth freedom,
    the empty-pocket Socialist innocence—
        making the rounds of cafes,
        coffee and ouzo, the marathon political talk,

your magnum opus New Deal art,
    the daily double at the track—
        With occasional upscale restaurant work,
        serving the glossy, good-tipping crowd

you despised. Who made poverty possible,
and bohemia better than home, a train ride away
in the land of chipped cups, uncut grass,
the uncomprehending child.

DOOR TO DOOR

We followed Tommy O'Toole, the iceman,
house to house, begging and grabbing chips,
ice slivers shaved from crystal blocks
brushed with the flavor of wood,
the flavor of the oak bed of Tommy's truck.

Back, it comes back in a rush,
the flavor of the neighborhood,
the cockadoodle of dawn,
the furry itch of tomato plants,
the yeasty reek of pond,

and the caravan of peddlers winding through:
George the milkman, Eddy the baker,
greengrocer Peppernill;
Fuller Brush man, scissors sharpener,
pots-pans-and-crockery man.

And Fritzy, who drove a dusty, low-slung,
dark-blue-faded-to-iridescence van,
and sold for a nickel
the quintessential, archetypal,
Platonic, vanilla ice cream cone.

RAGMAN

He wore the slump of a man grown weary
in his days, the slump
of tired clothes, of the rags he picked
and stuffed in his oily sack,

hooking its lip to the claw
of a hand held scale
and telling the weight from the heft,
without reading it.

His eyes were too small to find
in the knot of his face: heavy brows
and a nose beneath his cap,
and such teeth as never were brushed.

Whether he tried or not,
he never did smile when we asked
could we feed the horse.
We accepted a nod for a yes

and offered the beast an apple,
jibbing away from its hot nose-breath,
its rolling, gummy lip. And I wished
I were rich and could ransom it.

He gave us our nickel and having done
climbed like a scarecrow
up on his wagon and rumbled off,
soiling the road as he left.

THE PEOPLE OF SMOKE

Someone missing a chicken.
Another, a shirt off the line.
And the dogs barking at 2:00 AM.

They were here. They had come.
Encamped at the edge of town,
The people of smoke and shadow.

Of sleight of hand.
Of tambourine and violin.
Their colors—topaz and ruby,

Their colors—gold and blood.
They lived by Cup and Pentacle,
Sword and Wand, practiced in

The art of prophesy:
Gnomic of the crystal ball,
Runic of the palm,

The tea leaves' cryptogram.
Like smoke,
They came and were gone.

Where they had been
Stones sat in swarthy rings
And the grass lay down.

THE OLD TUFTS LIBRARY
Weymouth Landing
for Kate

Once the town had decided the old library must come down,
that its time had passed,
there was nothing to do but
                    carry it off intact
from the corner of Commercial and Washington
to the back lots of the affections,
                    remembering how it was . . .
Turret and arch—above the flat-roofed aspect of business,
ivy-veined walls alive across the brick with chittering sparrows,
that echo
                    in the meadows of the mind.
How the slightest breeze set the ivy rippling, turret to sidewalk,
with a dark water's shimmer that danced the length of the low fence
rimming the building,
                    setting it off
in a modest declaration of worth. A forged iron fence
that rang when struck with a stick, where in fall the leaves piled up
and where, at the end, lay the broken scatter of razed brick.
                    All that was left of . . .
times crossing the threshold, a decorous hush holding our voices
to a whisper, as in church; creeping on tiptoe to
                    the little wooden stools
in the turret corner window of the children's room.
Where we could look out at shoppers crossing the intersection
in the wan light of
                    a winter's afternoon,
watching for the snow to begin. And where in summer,
holding down the pages of
                    The Wind in the Willows
from the fan's cool droning breath, we went off with Mole and Rat
on a cross-country trek, and never looked back—
—Never looked back, as the days passed in rounds of
                    borrow and return.

WOODSMOKE

Like Mole, who felt the pull
of home beneath the grasses
as a wistfulness

before the message reached his brain
from the little mole heart,
the scent of woodsmoke on the evening

trips off some blind yearning
laid down in a ring of stones
before thought found tongue

or tongue words to reflect
what home and warmth
were to the body.

A primal trace, some nub of memory
the lobes have stored:
camps in the darkness,

a rude hearth, fire's hot blood
spilling out of the wood,
the good taste

of roasted flesh in the mouth,
warm, mealy roots,
the drowse that falls like a spell

when the belly is full.
Shaggy gusts of woodsmoke,
fingering the haze,

touch that place in us;
the banked embers ripple and snap
beneath their crust of snowy ash.

QUABBIN

I've been asked if people were angry
about losing their property in the takeover.
They weren't angry— They weren't angry people.
They were simply heartbroken.
                    —Sally Parker: Greenwich[1]

The mountains had no ambition to be islands.
The prisoned river never wished to climb them,
Swallowing roads that tied the villages and towns,
Flooding homes, displacing lives for this
Blue acreage spilling toward thirsty Boston.
Now deer and coyote browse and nose
The cellar holes along the shore,
Eagles fish where steeples caught the sun
In that lost valley twenty fathoms down.

With the first *Whereas,* what they feared had come.
Compliant, they went.
Over months and years, they went;
Slowly, as water drips. They took tulips and lilacs.
Gardens turned and picked, with their chickens they went.
With their hoes and scythes. They went with their beds
And books. Linens and lamps. Their dogs. Their cats.
All of the photographs.
The auctioneer handled the rest.

They left in trickles. Through a dozen years
The villages dwindled: Dana, Enfield, Greenwich, Prescott.
There were dead to transplant—bone, button, wedding ring.
In places no more than a dark shadow of soil
For the shovel to kiss and lift, generations of families:
A resurrection of the blood.

The letters slid in like mud:
        You are hereby notified that the Commonwealth
        of Massachusetts acting through its Metropolitan
        District Water Supply Commission requires on
        April 1, 1938, the land and buildings now occupied
        by you. . . .

Most, by April, had already gone. To Ware. To Athol.
To Belchertown . . . An exodus begun with the first *Whereas*—
Whereas they were few and far,
Whereas Boston were many and more,
Whereas for the *public convenience* . . .
—A bowl to fill the cup of *public convenience*.

When spring came looking for trees to green,
It would bypass those logged lanes and woodlots.
Nothing but stumps and stones where forest had been.
Nothing but mud and dust and the brave face of a dandelion
As the great dam spread over the ravaged land
And the last day dawned. With stoic grace
They faced the end of the known. Neighbors returned
for a final parting, the Enfield Firemen's Farewell Ball:
The Valley would dance its last moments.

J. R. Greene puts down:
How black draped horses led the old fire engine
        to the town hall door;
How the building was hung in patriotic bunting,
        red-white-and-blue trimmed with black;
How they'd planned for three hundred
        but a thousand squeezed in
        with twice that many outside;
How Trudy Ward Stalbird returned from upstate
        wearing her wedding gown
        and a velvet jacket of black;
How at the stroke of midnight, the band played
        Auld Lang Syne;
How the last song sung was *Home Sweet Home.*[2]

[1] Florentine Films, *The Old Quabbin Valley* (1981).

[2] J. R. Greene, *The Day Four Quabbin Towns Died* (1985).

KRAMER'S FARM

Shouldering
out of the ground fog,
the silo,
diaphanous as a dream,
round
with the warm promise
of enough.

Silo and barn,
castle and keep
of my country:
this is what we were
before the dream blurred.

LIMINAL

TIDAL MARSH

All cats are *she* from a distance.
This one's pretty body
combs the blond hair of the marsh,
scattering crows.
The sickled paw swipes.
From here it seems a game—
the mouse torn from its thatch
of grasses, naked tail
hanging slack.

Here is where the sea comes
to weep in the mother grasses.
The iron cold Atlantic
runs home twice a day
to the great lap,
and the marsh gathers
the broken waters
into herself.

STONY BROOK LANE

In Memory of Marguerite Burbank

Letting the afternoon
    slide past
        like an outbound boat

on the river,
    forgetting time
        in the reach of thought,

our quiet talks
    about the improbability
        of any world beyond

this given one
    of measured season—
        If you were there

I would come
    and sit with you,
        watching the birds

scatter the seeds
    of your largess
        across the porch,

facing the wind
    sweeping the marsh
        and fingering

the slow-leafing
    ironwood tree.
        If you were there

spring would be again
    your bright face
        among the geraniums.

THE ROCK LADY

for Sylvia

"Where do you get such stones?"
"I import them—from Italy."

She finds them where they fell in woods and fields,
crumbs from the glacier's munching
in its slow slide south.

Some she harvests in her garden, sunk among
the edibles like petrified potatoes.
Most are gathered

from the Nantasket littoral, helter-skelter masonry
of storm, of ocean's finicky
dissatisfaction

with everything the way it was and is.
She goes there as to the grocer,
her critical eye

panning the shingle for something promising—
the quick scan and then the close
examination:

the peering, picking, the hefting in palm,
the turning round, the pause
as if listening

for some exchange between the self and stone
to recommend it to the discipline
of her hand.

What she carries home will be her canvas.
What they have said to one another
will be art.

Nantasket Beach

November 1979

Night comes over the ocean,
the sand, the November arcade.
A girl is juggling three batons.

A plane noses down toward Logan.
The roller coaster, a great wave
on the skyline.

The sand, printed over
with the hand of the ocean.
A tanker cuts the horizon.

A girl is juggling.
The dying sun is a burning baton,
a leaf fire, a lamp shade

lighting the inn.

NIGHT VISION

Headlights against the seawall
send shadow animals scurrying,
flat and eyeless
in their gray stone fur.
This is their breeding time,
clowder and gang,
late summer nights,
slinking between cars,
looking for their kind.

Over there,
full and orange-round,
what a moon should be,
and the whole coastline
to play with.
The soft sprawl of bluff
a drowsy city,
dreamy, moon-marked land
of Saturdays and sleep.

SPREAD OF WAVES

A red sun dallies
in the west,
like a moon in heat.

Reports of guns
sound the distance
from shoreline trees
misted suave as felt.

Darkness hovers lower
in the island of reeds
and nests in the blind
the hunters fixed.

We raise anchor.
Paired crabs
release each other.

Do you not think
a woman knows desire
in the billowing air
flushing her blouse,

in the spread of waves
amethyst and mauve
against the prow?

SALT POND

You led me to the great salt pond,
and pointing to the farther shore
said, *There they are—the swans.*
The pair surrounded by their little ones,
I could not see how many.
Anyway, it was a family.
This is paradise, you said.

The sheltered pond, the swans,
the sea behind us—
Who would not want to live like this?
Nibbling rose hips at sunset,
Venus a spark in the flaming sky,
one with the swans;

watching them
trundle the great feathered pods
of their bodies onto the damp grasses,
night coming on, settling into dream,
a pair together.

HERRING RUN

Having come this far out of the Atlantic
and up the Back River, they pause,
recovering strength for the final plunge
toward Whitman's amber waters
that spread above the falls of Iron Hill:
the cradle from which they came,
where they in turn will spawn.

They must climb three ladders yet,
past pairs of grappling hands,
a paradigm of the hero's journey:
the ritual return,
the perilous path,
the triune test of courage.

Sleek and dark, round and round
they churn, biding time,
gathering numbers,
gathering momentum;
all their light folded beneath,
shown livid and tinny in death.

One, then another, breaks from the swarm,
facing into the sluice,
the down-rushing crush of water.
The ordeal begun,
it advances by dart, by leap,
forced back time and again.

Time and again
thrusting the small glistening sword of its body
forward,
until the whole whorling numberless mass
has passed the gauntlet—
a dark galaxy
whipped on by a single commandment.

BACK RIVER

In the brisk wind, the April sun fell like a shawl
on my back and on the aluminum gunwales
warming my hands. The canoe slid along the banks
the river carved through the marsh,
sitting so low with the tide
we steered among a density of root,
a thatched palisade where sea things clung,
mussels and periwinkles matted in,
heavy with a low-tide stench,
the rack and rot of mudflat life.
A heron rose grandly up from the Hingham shore,
threading its shadow over reeds and water
to Weymouth. Farther up, on the esker,
the trees were afire with waxwings,
the first I'd ever seen. And not one,
not a mating pair alone, a clamoring colony of them,
all tawny and rose, feathers like
fragments of sunset—cardinals in tie-dye.

This was the maiden voyage, the christening
of the Grumman, a sixteen-foot, keel bottom version
of the birchbark craft in art-nouveau frames
lodged in my imagination
among words as familiar and strange as
Massachusetts, Narragansett. I had wanted a canoe
more than the antique Bokhara at the auction,
more than the Eastlake marble-top dry sink.
A canoe— To get out of the house,
to get close to the brown scruff of the muskrat
plowing its noiseless wake,
the stiff, deliberate strut of the egret.
I wanted to get close.
Close enough to earn the insults of the territorial crows,
to sit on the salt tongue of the marsh
when the wind spoke, and feel all around me
the Algonquin earth naming the place: Wessagusset.

STRAWBERRY POINT
for Marilou

We would come late to the beach
where the tide eddies in from Minot's Light,
our shadows thrown over sand
as one long shadow,
and find a spot on the Point's stone chin
to watch the sun set,
listening to the waves lap,
sharing the concerns of the young.

Letting our thoughts float off
on the gilt wash of dissolving rim
until everything was swallowed
in shadow, then make our way back.
Two shadows
skirting pools of silvered light,
where what hangs on the tide
lives, for as long as it lasts, by luck.

Now, this shadow fear . . .
My friend, you stumble on the stair,
shrink from the gathering dark,
huddle in my embrace.
I want to get you out of this sick place
to the rocks off Minot,
sit with you in silhouette:
two women, rising out of stone,

neither flesh nor earth.

WEYMOUTH LANDING

When I am carrying the weight
of a great anchor inside myself,
I go down to the wall at the Landing,
where the moist stones wear the colors
of what is not water, the moist stones
with their iron stains,
built into and out of the river,
built to hold back the land,
like buttoned police,
that the boats may pass.

I come for the boats,
wait as if my ship were due.
From a sort of pinnacle
among the mounded stones,
hail the setters-out and the lee-bound.
It is a good place to wait,
to be thrilled at whatever comes.

Eels are down there, turning, turning,
convolutions as terrible to imagine
as the serpents entwining Laocoön,
if as a child you had caught one
at twilight, lifted, and known it
for the heart of all darkness
writhing from your line.

When you have lived most of your life
near water, for all its terrors
there is no other comforter,
and you return just to be there
looking outward, faceless
as the tresses of eelgrass.

OCEANIC

This is why we come here:

The need to be less
than a footprint
sunk in sand;

stone deaf
to the gathering waters,
the tongues of the foam;

blind
to what the sun does
with light;

to ascend into heaven
all and at once,
the salt breath of the place.

INVITATION

The grass need not be tall
to take you in. To enter

the intimate separateness
of each clean blade

you need not sprawl upon
or kneel on it.

You needn't be competent,
or moral, or anything.

Let the eye run freely along
and the grass says, yes.

LIMINAL

Transparent as wind,
it moves among weeds,
where they melt into marsh
and blend with the amber broth
of the pond.

I have glimpsed it in stillness
through the black grate
of winter trees
where the last light bled
from a luminous gash in the sky.

I have stood at the crest
of a granite ledge
and felt the thing
stirring beneath in its burrow,
its covert of shadow.

The tenant of shadow
it enters the room,
keeping its counsel
without promise or reproach.
It has come as close

as the echo of my step
in the jeweled twilight
of an empty chapel,
exciting the candles, casting a blush
on the Virgin's pale foot.

All my life it has hidden its face,
hovering just out of reach—
a dragonfly skimming the pond
as if it were lost
at the door of its home.

LILACS

Lilacs, remembered
blooming in evening tones,
shedding sun
and dappling porches,

scenting rooms within the reach
of wooden stairs,
their perfume rising
with the fillip of a curtain.

Lilacs, shadowed in the scent
of a linen handkerchief
held against the breast.
The same in chambers

above the shingle
and sea-wrack of the storm,
mixed with salt and flotsam
—lilacs.

SHADOWED IN THE POND

You live
in warm folds of memory,
cradled

in lilacs,
in the little white bells
of lily-of-the-valley.

I am a study of you
shadowed in the pond;
my life streams out of yours.

I see you wringing sheets,
like white clouds scrubbed
and rinsed in clear blue light,

your small hands cracked
as leaves in winter.
You gardened on days like this.

You filled the house
with sheaves of purple iris
while I found places to hide

and sit like a rooted tree
until the warm smell of supper
called with your voice.

WHITMAN'S POND

Whitman's Pond was where I learned
    you could make friends with water
        but it might turn on you,
take your breath and never give it back.

I wasn't any more careful—but I was luckier
    than Billy. (A whole lot luckier than
        Grace Asquith; police
dragging the pond with grappling hooks.)

Whitman's Pond was the color of ale.
    It took on a reasty smell in summer,
        the smell of snail and sunfish
and leaky cesspool.

I swam there anyway and never caught polio.
    It was Lake Placid in winter, when I
        was Sonja Henie in her laced-up
white skates custom made at Clapp Shoe.

And in spring when the herring ran,
    I stood on the footbridge and watched them
        come over the falls to spawn.
And I was the shaman

whose prayer had brought them, whose song
    had urged them, whose dance
        had drawn them out of the Atlantic.
Each year proved it to be so: the gift, in trust,

to the child who watched and listened
    where long fingers of light
        combed the woods, stroked the pond,
and ushered the new life in.

THE STONE BRIDGE
for Reed

His little girls
   give him fishing lures
      for the tackle box
         his father left.
         That was Grampy's,
   Jennifer says.
  Heather insists
she remembers him.
Kendra, the newborn,
   sleeps tucked in the lore
      of her namesake.
         Their father,
           listening past them,
      hears the cry
  of redwings
riding marsh reeds
across a drizzle of Aprils
   to the stone bridge
      where the stream
         reels out of a pool
         stocked with trout.
   His own dad there
on the opposite shore,
pleased, impressed,
lured by its promise
   down the slick descent,
      the pool's dark peace
         unwrapping
         in glints and flashes:
      trout, banked against
   the pull of the stream,
turning, returning.

STUDY IN BLACK AND WHITE

for Laurel

The woman who holds the little girl's hand
was young then. The stone,
in late September light, looks warm.

The wall of the sluice,
a foot or two above the shallow run,
proved a good place to stand

for the full effect of shadow
and sun pouring down
on the low falls, the dazzling stream.

Almost audible to me now
the rush of water sweeping past
the merged shadows of child and mother

flowing as one across the plunging river.
Child leans into mother, who clasps
her daughter's hand in her own.

From the angle of her body,
you see the little girl is relaxed.
Her mother stands at wall end, braced,

where it drops in line with the falls.
A long blade of light scissors the platform,
silhouetting them as in a radiance.

The scene is soft. A gentle muting
in the reproduction of the photograph
gives a smoky effect,

the image old mirrors throw back.

IT IS SEPTEMBER

It is September now
and I have not been
to the woods.

I have not been
to the woods,
where the swan of my blood

is loosed.
The swan of my blood,
its great wings

hard in my breast,
its long throat
mute

with the unuttered word,
its one word,
the wild cry—*home.*

It is September
and I have not been
to the lakes of reflection.

FOX CREEK

From my day of inventorying the field work
of the hunters and gatherers of stone tools

from a lost time that left no name of its own—
saying that Dalton, Kirk, Brewerton and like

tell only what the tongues of our own time
happen upon—it was in passing

beneath the descendants of trees
that gave branch and limb to the hafting

of those wrought stones, the flaked and notched
flint, chert, quartz that accomplished

the ancient stalkers' work, that I saw
the wild figure of the fox like a hunted thing,

fur-fletched tail straight as an arrow,
dash from cover to green cover across the road

where I passed in the leaf light of late afternoon
through which the stream ran.

HINGHAM AMMUNITION DEPOT

Ghostly now, these storage places,
traces of the war
we buried here. Concrete
pasted over with autumn colors,
camouflage of oak and maple
dappling the mossy walls.

Fall's a good time to savor
the peace of these old bunkers,
where the past hunkers down
and the last warmth of the year
digs in, holding on as if color
were an arsenal against cold:

Gold of birch and aspen,
the bold advance of scarlet hawthorn,
before November's monotone
takes all this territory,
claimed for cold
and held against all human will.

It will go gray,
gray as Forties combat film,
the walls of these old installations
shown in all their stark abandonment,
like burned-out, bombed-out towns
where nothing moves but shadow and wind.

NOCTURNE

for Jennifer, Heather, and Kendra

The trees have thrown their blue hush
across the lawn. Across the way
Mrs. Norris has gone in.
It is that time between time

when swallows play in the painted corners
of the light and the children on the lawn
linger, climb upon the old dog:
old, arthritic dog.

How patient he is with these
who hug so furiously his old dog neck,
clamber over the old bone of his back,
until their father comes

scooping up plums from the lawn.
They squeal and gang. They counterattack,
a fusillade from the fecund plum,
which stops as suddenly as it began.

And the old dog follows them in.

NIGHT PIECE

Now the sky holds all its light
to throw at the leashed darkness,
and trees keep back their breath.
Noise of the street is farther off,
low and farther off,
and overhead a plane hums.

Crickets wake in the grass
and ferns rise up,
ferns rise up,
trees fold down,
fold down, and in
a soft green envelope
sleep comes.

OLD GODS

BIRTHDAY

Morning comes burning out of night,
the orange moon high in the south
torching the trees,
the grove stifled in mist,
and all the hidden creatures
on the smoking earth
twisting with lust.

The crow calls.
The lotus bursts.

WEED

What you did not expect to see,
the broadleafed weed
rising in the garden,

prominent among fern and ivy,
laurel and rhododendron:
those desirable forms.

Spiraling, rivaling these,
something the rain invited—
Rain that relaxes intention,

aiding diversity,
the green urge
to surprise.

SKUNK CABBAGE

Mother of the wild and gamey reek,
it bores through snow.

It melts the puddled ice in sloughs and swamps
with its own green heat.

Before you hear the peepers' pulsing trill,
the mottled green and livid-purple spathe

accomplishes its urgent loamy thrust,
seizing light and throwing off a redolence

so rankly acrid it assails the nostrils,
offending glands adapted more for fragrance.

Cabbagey and elephantine, these leaves splay
emphatically to occupy their boggy ground.

This is a plant that wants to be alone
with its kind, private in its element.

It would perish in a proper garden.

PLUM

Everything that flowers
flowers for itself.
The flesh of the plum
swells sweet,
capsuled in its royal wrap.
All that preparation

just to be.

And when I have finished,
nothing left
but the liberated seed,
green tongue coiled within,
waiting for a chance
to taste the bitten earth.

THE FERLIE ONES

They were everywhere
        in summer,
the ferlie ones
        in their beautiful skins,
sliding under the porch

a breath from my foot
        when I left the house,
spilling from the shaved lawn
        into the ditch
as I ran past barefoot.

Trespassers,
        hiding their underparts
as they fled back
        to the narrow dark
from which they'd come:

black, brown, yellow,
        stripe and pattern,
some green as stems
        extruded into sun
through cracks and crevices.

You might meet one
        on any wooded path,
a root losing itself
        faster
than your imagination.

You knew what you saw
        but couldn't be sure,
the signature of a terror
        that had nothing to do
with venom.

It was the way they moved.
        It was the flinty eye
and pasty belly,
        the smiling gash of the face,
its flickering tongue.

I could not bear to look
      at them.
And yet, bewitched,
      I watched
the garter peel back

the sleeve of its old self
      and wriggle off
leaving in its place
      a silvery tube of slough
shucked smooth

as a sheath of cellophane,
      only the luster
of its host left.
      Passive, approachable,
with nothing to deflect

my intent, the shed skin
      invited study—
but my curious hand
      shrank back,
as if a presence lingered.

Walking the road, I'd pass
      the wracked coils of those
that never made it across,
      iridescent scrolls
pressed on the soft tar

—letters
      of an alien alphabet—
the ferlie ones
      who fled from me,
as I from them.

And now I seldom see one
      out in the open,
though they nest
      below the stones
of dreams.

CHICKENS

I had learned to hate chickens:
their one-eyed spite,
their strutting cannibalism,
but I loved to scatter their grain
from my hand. So when I fed them
it was to please myself alone.

Creaking open the hinged lid,
digging my hand through fathoms
of the dusty, billowy mass,
I would bury my arm to the elbow
and dredge up a fistful
of the gritty spill
to let it run smoking
through my fingers.

I would fling the next handful
as far from myself as possible
and watch the scabby creatures
run after it in the meanness
of their gullet lust,
squawking and scrabbling
over the sour earth.

THE OTTER

She toils across the compass of her pool,
each time pushing off
with her little leather-mittened foot,
plowing meters in a trough
for the kiss and snub of cement.
Blind as a cloud she tumbles
over gray concrete and scattered coins
that glint in the sun
like a school of startled minnows—

Like minnows in ponds,
the weedy ponds
of perch and prowling bullhead,
of crayfish scanning the murk;
lakes
of grazing bass and pickerel,
of swoop and lunge—

Round she wheels and back she comes
doing her laps, a large brown slub
shuttling to and fro on a watery loom;
the strong claws,
for guddling eel and bottom fish,
folded against her flesh in a tumbling act
more like the pacing of the great, caged cats.

Cut off from the life of the river
and held in the pull
of its branching limbs and serried skin
sliding pollen-scummed
down the chute and spill of rapids,
the halls and alleys of trout.

TITICUT
(Great River)

Before she was the "Taunton," she was Titicut;
the name comes off the tongue like birdsong.
Flat and warm, with the mud smell rivers sweat,
she slides big bellied through Pocanoket country,
crossing Taunton, Dighton, Swansea . . .

rolling out, swallowing the smaller streams,
drinking salt the tide brings up from Mt. Hope Bay,
whose *bitter waters* take her to the sea.
Blowzy June catalpas bunched on the larboard bank
scatter their honeyed blossoms over the river's slack

in dewy stars the launch disperses as we pass.
Turtles abandon basking logs in abrupt plops.
Here—there—a snaky cormorant neck upthrusts,
bodiless. Clouds swim alongside, shaping, reshaping,
keeping up with our chugging craft

that plows a course midstream between
the green entanglements resisting towns
whose day had not yet come when the river
was a Wampanoag highway dugouts plied
in the bastion of their wilderness.

Here, Weetamoo, queen of the Pocassets,
plunged from her raft and drowned,
the Plymouth men closing in
—those godfearing men—
who displayed her head on a pole in Taunton.

Through guilt, remorse, the toxins of neglect,
Titicut bears on. We see osprey nesting
on platforms the agricultural school put up.
With the mills gone, the river is coming back.
Left to herself, she may remember who she was.

OLD GODS

Evening brings a good kind of tired, earned
walking the woods behind the abandoned
County Hospital you love, with a deep sad
love, and I, for reasons beyond memory.

Something quite apart from the ten-year
suffered loss of a father to TB—the son
standing below the unapproachable man
in the window, waving. Something elusive

this old tile-and-stucco shrine evokes,
not antiquity so much as timelessness.
There is an aura here not unlike
the melancholy peace of cemeteries.

And, it's one of the last good places left
to walk, to feel the press of the foot
on earth, leaves, twigs, small stones,
moss, the rangy uncut grass—and mud,

the voluptuous squish of mud.
The path between the bog and pond
is strewn with litter jettisoned in fern
and teaberry. We bend to the task,

gather up as much as we can carry.
Disentangling a length of fishing line
from a low branch, a silver birch
the setting sun tints carmine,

you raise a hand, warning me back
from the black racer coiled in ground pine,
torpid having eaten. Above, a brazen red-tail,
perceiving opportunity, calculates the risk.

We leave them to their fierce and honeyed work,
old gods who keep the seasons in hives of wilderness.

SILVERBACK

Like a toy a child might have dropped
falling off to a nap, the skunk
lay on its side in the street
in a slice of February sun,
paw pads printing
the moment of misstep.
No blood.
No visible lacerations.

A perfect Steiff,
but for the spilled stink of skunk
staining the morning,
the teeth of the jaw
ajar in the smile of a knife
that would if it could
rip a finger up.
Nothing worked—

The little snout
would never rouse again
to the edible thrills
of the kingdom.
But beautiful,
the way the mantle fur
drifted down the dark flanks
in an ermine snow.

I pushed it with a stick
from the shoulder into the leaves,
then under the leaves, covering it.
And went on downwind,
breathing skunk in, taking it
oxygen warm to the lungs.

WESTON PARK
February 23, 1979

They have felled the trees
and leveled the hill.

They have filled the hollow
the ferlie god made.

All of what they could not see
they buried

where the rain water lived.
No one can walk here anymore.

Everywhere the water weeps,
looking for its own place.

SHAGBARK

Not a pretty tree,
it is grandly shabby, inhabiting its name,
the long throat of itself spoken of earth.

Self-contained,
lone and tall at the edge of the wood,
trailing its ragged cloak

through the blue smoke of autumn;
shedding bark, leaf, a hard-shelled fruit
husked in pungent rind.

Magnificent in moonlight,
half tree, half animal,
rampant shadow of the wood.

Hair-shirt flagellant
when the wind comes
full of its own ragged breath,

the leaf-stripper
ripping pages of October
twig from limb, thrown

to the mercy of the grass
with the hatched nut nested in its rind,
spanked green and blighted brown.

Burst crescents
staining the nail with tannin,
astringent, burnt-lime,

a taste that sings on the tongue.
And the sweet, chambered meat
at the nugget's heart.

THE POLE YARD

Weymouth Light & Power Company
Iron Hill Street

I have seen the great hard pines
without arms,
row on row
racked in the sun,
each waiting its turn
to return to the sky:
to return as a spine,
never to bend,
never to quicken,
never to hush the rain,
never to smell of pine.

I have seen the giants,
bled of pitch
and mystery,
oozing creosote
like asphalt,
and the old ones powdering,
and the black ants winding
in and out of the sun.

APRIL

Her hand is everywhere today,
unwrapping the dogwood,
the cherry ...

Winter long, she huddled
in the stoic sparrow
clutching the brittle limb.

Taciturn, listening
for the sound of ice releasing,
the sliding down of rain.

WOOD THRUSH

Flute like—
from woods behind the house

heard, or seen scratching in leaves
blown in and about dry-rot logs

and scrap lumber
thrown against the shaded garage,

old, ramshackle, that seemed
to have grown slapdash up

from the weathered pile of neglect
at its feet

—the chestnut bird,
color of flaking brown paint

sifting into leaves pressed
and folded one upon another

like the feathered song
in the spotted, white breast

that sprang out of camouflage
up from the ground.

A PLACE IN THE WOODS

Nowhere in the whole whiskered world
was moss so furry green,
so soft and undulant,

so cushioning to the step.
A carpet of plush
that drew me barefoot

around the ring of summer,
flexing underfoot, exciting the skin,
returning my touch.

The way the light behaved,
lambent,
flickering across the surface,

emerald
as the prized gem stone
crushed to fairy fire and woven;

light
felt as a shiver in the bone
shone on the moss.

And the way it took my foot,
disquieting,
sawing with velvet teeth

at the nerve ends.

MUSHROOMS

Two that have gloomed
where nothing was,
bred out of earth
on ichor and fust,
bloodless white.

Blind beggars on stumps,
airy with prophesy,
witnessing against the light
a closure complete
and irrevocable,

a faceless blossoming.

EFFIGY

A stone
and more than a stone,
I gave him the name of *Bog*.

He had taken it upon himself,
immersed to his neck.
A face emerging from its pit

with the look of exquisite pain
only a god could know.
—A god out of myth

who had transgressed.
Pushed out of heaven.
Cursed. Buried in earth.

Trodden.
A face looking up,
broken.

That I freed from its prison,
that I placed in the sun
of my garden.

BEFORE THE RAIN

Only a squirrel threading among limbs
moves the morning.
Rain is in the air.

November has wrapped its gray wool
over the house, the yard.
Dogs, kids, cars, smothered in hush.

Not a bird troubles the firebush.
Yesterday
the lawn people were here

harrying the leaves
with their blowing machines.
Gone are the rakers with their long arms

and simple prongs.
The quiet rakers, the boisterous leaves,
the smoldering incense of autumn—gone.

IN A LIGHT RAIN

It is raining,
and there is a fire
at the edge of the field.

Fire in the long blond grass
at the edge of the field,
nibbling through rain.

It is a small fire in a small field
of the great world
that turns on the spit of the sun.

We have seen fires—
thousand-acre woodlands
burning,

smoke and flame blocking the sun,
baking the ground,
ponds turning to steam.

And the animals.
The animals.
The animals.

Where there is wind
fire takes it, wears it,
makes it its own.

The boned trees,
houses, humans,
and the animals.

Fire is our first fear:
Don't touch—Hot!
If we were to move in close,

we would hear the fire's voice,
the dry munch of it eating its food,
leaving the tougher parts.

NOVEMBER MORNING

Gray cloud light
smoking over the mountain,
day up on its haunches:

First the trees.
Then the grass.
Crow's sharp cry.

Bird answering bird.
Everything drinks rain,
late greening lawn

and wizzled root,
the red-berry bush
on Pine Glen—

Here before road and houses,
here with the look
of what has always been.

Wild red-berry bush,
worm at worm's blind labor,
crow chipped out of the dark:

each thing engaged and distant.

INDIAN SUMMER

After four days of rain, the copper beech
still holds a thatch thick enough to shelter
scores of anonymous birds. The ash is stripped.
The lawn is covered with downed leaves from the maples,
glistening in wet light, strewn in a trail to the woods,
the great lodge where the old wise one lives. This
is his time, this sanguine turn.

Four days and four nights, while the raccoon crouched
in her den and the pond crept up to the alder
and gray birch along the bank, he stood with the trees,
becoming root, opening himself to the rain.
Now he comes in a sweat of sweetfern and humus.

I smell his pipe through the mist. I can almost see
his brown veined skin, his scruffy cloak spread
over the ground, the tamped loamy earth of the path
down to the pond, and the half-moons of his eyes
squinting across into the night, conjuring
the yellow-eyed owl, the silver canoe trembling
on the water's glass face.

My blood picks up the rhythm of his chant:
song of the bird trolling the dark,
song of the tree taking joy in its solitary body,
song of the self wrapped in the tight bone house.

THE EVENHANDED RAIN

The evenhanded rain falls softly
over grass and stone
and on the backs of the solemn beasts,
the patient beasts,
who press their patient bones
close to the earth.

This is the way of beasts.
This is the way of rain.
This is the comfort of earth.

DEER IN THE RAIN

When I found the tamped place of their night
pressed upon fern,
I had hoped they would come.

Rain wet, faces prettily alert, the doe and her fawn
stepped out of the trees,
pausing to browse beside the deck

in ground cover of myrtle and ivy.
Their tawny coats rain-slicked,
hairs etched into detail in the gray light.

Unable to move on my side of the glass
without breaking the spell,
and no way to welcome, I waited,

watching them eat, working slowly back
toward the trees,
until the white flags of their rumps

were inked out by hemlock.

WOLF

We hear
you have returned
unseen to the forest,

dispersed in stillness.
Your song
above the forest hush,

your paw print in snow
tracking the bald spaces,
the sheltering dense.

Curious, cautious
absinthe eye, glimpsed
in flight through balsam.

Your welcome
is a dubious thing,
a truce brittle as dry twig.

There may never be
forgiveness between us,
your kind do not beg.

WILDERNESS

This place has no nakedness,
filling itself with the seasons.
The rocks arrange themselves for leisure.
The trees work at their own pace.
The ponds collect a depth.

We say the day is raw and cold.
The day dismisses us,
retreating into the reeds, the pines,
the frost-burnt mosses, the day
with its roots in winter now,
in the old, slow growth.

Lovely because it is empty.

BOG ICE

I've had such dreams of narrowing,
of danger closing in, losing
the ground that kept me as I ran.

In that dark light I saw the swans
peddling in circles, feathers to the wind,
a sharp wind that may have helped

hold back the pincer progress of ice,
though it seemed a torment to them,
bearing down upon the pair,

stranded in that desolate place.
Black, blue-black the face of the pool,
collared in spiny lace.

WHAT THE STORM PROVES

A fierce contest the giant fir
has with the wind,
the wind buffeting, caterwauling,
seizing and flinging the snow.

The fir writhing and flailing,
its dark body an agony of greatness.
How it endures, has endured
through all the unpromised years,

roots in their dark sleep
full of hints and rumors
where the sap waits,
like a stanched wound eager to bleed.

TEMENOS

Whipping blizzards out of the low boughs
and spoiling the snow underfoot,
we made it to the overlook
as the sun burned
lavishly down
to a purple
end,

spilling gold along the seams of the clouds,
washing a luminous grace over us
and the dark man in scarlet
who came toward us
through the trees
as softly as
a bird.

"I'm David," he said. —A spirit of the wood
offering his name and his hand.
Snow pearled the black wool
of his beard, glistened
on olive-black skin,
and his eyes
shone

with the soft blossoming light that dapples
the stillness of ponds. A dazzle
that calmed and held,
shaping, reshaping,
kaleidoscoping
arabesques
of form:

fish, flowers, animals, trees, and stones,
mites of things so small thousands
clustered on a single petal,
like spinning galaxies.
All this swept past,
the vision of a
second.

I blinked and spoke out loud the thought
that broke the spell: bodhisattva.
His smile broke into a laugh,
and we left it at that.
He would stay at
the cabin till
January,

away from the town. We left him there,
a spear of flame in the dying light,
facing the wind, and returned
through hemlock, boughs
zippering together
softly as we
passed.

ABOUT THE AUTHOR

Faye George is the author of two chapbooks and the book-length collection *A Wound on Stone* (Perugia Press, 2001). She has received the Arizona Poetry Society's Memorial Award, the New England Poetry Club's Gretchen Warren Award and Erika Mumford Prize. Her poems have appeared in distinguished literary and naturalist journals, anthologies, and periodicals: *The Paris Review, Poetry, Sanctuary, Yankee. . .* She is represented in *Poetry* magazine's 90th year retrospective, *The Poetry Anthology, 1912-2002*. A native of Weymouth, Massachusetts, Faye has lived in Connecticut, Rhode Island, New Hampshire and Virginia, and now makes her home in Bridgewater, Massachusetts. She has a son, a daughter, and granddaughters, in Virginia and Connecticut.